IMAGES
of America

OSSABAW ISLAND

This map of Ossabaw Island shows the many tidal creeks that flow in and out of Ossabaw's vast marshlands. (Courtesy of Eleanor Torrey West, private collection.)

The photograph on the cover is courtesy of Paul Efird.

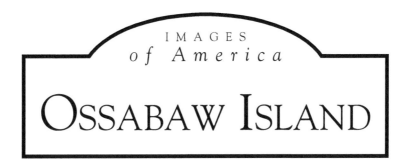

IMAGES
of America

OSSABAW ISLAND

Ann Foskey

ARCADIA
PUBLISHING

Published by Arcadia Publishing
Charleston, South Carolina

Library of Congress Catalog Card Number: 2001087663

For all general information contact Arcadia Publishing at:
Telephone 843-853-2070
Fax 843-853-0044
E-mail sales@arcadiapublishing.com
For customer service and orders:
Toll-Free 1-888-313-2665

Visit us on the Internet at www.arcadiapublishing.com

DEDICATION

To the Spirit of Wild Places, so powerfully experienced on Ossabaw, that quickens us, and reminds us that we are a part of this magnificent creation called Earth.

4

CONTENTS

ACKNOWLEDGMENTS

On behalf of all who read and enjoy this book, I would like to thank Eleanor Torrey West and William Ford Torrey Jr., who generously shared their family's Ossabaw photograph albums, which formed the primary source and inspiration for this project. Thanks also go to Jeffrey J. Carmel for scanning and submitting photographs from the photo albums of his mother, Patricia Schlotman Carmel, chronicling Ossabaw Island in the late 1920s and 1930s.

Many thanks go to the staff of the Georgia Historical Society, especially Mandi Johnson and Susan Dick for their assistance with this project and Lisa White, former president of the Georgia Historical Society, for suggesting that this book be written.

Special acknowledgment goes to the Historic Preservation Division of the Georgia Department of Natural Resources, especially historian Ken Thomas, who wrote the nomination for Ossabaw Island's listing in the National Register of Historic Places. The nomination form is the source of much of the early history provided in this book and includes earlier work by Beth Lattimore Reiter and Marilyn Pennington, as well as an extensive bibliography documenting the research. The Historic Preservation Division regularly updates the Ossabaw file with new discoveries in the island's history and pre-history.

For the chapters representing the activities of the Ossabaw Foundation, I wish to thank the following artists, without whose involvement this book would be incomplete: John Earl, Emily Earl, Helen Hamada, Al Bradford, and Paul Efird. Thanks also to Dr. M. Craig Allee for sharing his photographs and for maintaining the tradition of Shorter College coastal ecology field study on Ossabaw for 32 years (and counting). Thanks to Elrod Sims for resurrecting and scanning the Ellen Biddle Shipman landscape plans. Thanks also to Clifford West, Cyrus Martin Jr., William Haynes, and Fred Johnson for sharing recollections of life on and around Ossabaw Island. Thank you also to Katie White and the staff of Arcadia Publishing for their assistance in editing and printing the book.

This project could not have happened without a great support team on the home front. Thanks to my parents, Bill and Nancy Newman, for their love and support and for providing back-up babysitting many a time. (And thanks, Mom, for saving all those newspaper clippings that kept me in touch with Ossabaw over the years.) Thanks to my mother-in-law and friend Marilyn Foskey, for her encouragement and humor, and for being a woman of strength and an inspiration to me; to my sister Mary Hoag, for her enthusiastic support across the miles; to my sister, Jane Newman Jackson, for her encouragement and help with William; and to the great moms of Village Montessori School of Roswell, especially Patricia Hovater, Robyn Pinto, Kathy Hankinson, and Liz Gillespie, for watching William in the afternoons during my frequent trips to the island. Thanks also to Joan Newton, for encouraging me to make the call that brought me back to Ossabaw after 20 years, to Daniel Price, for helping keep the kindred spirits of Ossabaw in touch, and to Beth and Andrew Adams for their friendship and hospitality in providing a home base in Savannah. And finally, thanks to my son William, for being a partner in this adventure, and to my husband John Foskey, for his love, support, patience, encouragement, technical know-how, and sense of humor through all the stages of this project.

INTRODUCTION

Ossabaw Island is one in a chain of barrier islands located along the southeastern coast of the United States. The island lies approximately seven miles by water south of Savannah, Georgia. It is bounded by the Ogeechee River on the north, the Atlantic Ocean on the east, St. Catherine's sound on the south, and the Intracoastal Waterway on the west. One of Georgia's largest barrier islands, Ossabaw is made up of 9,000 acres of forested uplands with freshwater ponds and 16,000 acres of marshlands interlaced with tidal creeks. There are no bridges or causeways linking the island to the mainland.

Along Ossabaw's creeks, oyster shell middens littered with pottery shards mark the presence of small seasonal villages dating to 4,000 years ago, when the island's earliest human inhabitants gathered food from the marshes and tidal creeks. Over the millenia, native cultures evolved to include agriculture, larger and more permanent villages, more centralized political units, and more elaborate burial customs. Several burial mounds were investigated on Ossabaw in 1896 by Clarence Moore, who published his findings in the book, *Certain Aboriginal Mounds of the Georgia Coast*.

By the time of Spanish exploration of the eastern coast of North America in the early 1500s, it was the Guale Indians who inhabited most of the Georgia coast. The Guale were a distinct cultural group of Muskogean language stock. Investigations of pre-mission Guale sites on the coast revealed evidence of maize farming, but also a reliance on gathering, as shown by acorns, hickory nuts, persimmons, and grapes. Spanish missionaries altered the Guale practices from food gathering to a dependence on food production. This led the Guale to concentrate in more sedentary villages, where they grew food for themselves and for the missions and garrisons of the Spanish. Periodically throughout the mission period, the Guale rebelled in response to excessive Spanish demands and the Spanish retaliated by attacking and burning villages and destroying stored food. In 1579 the Indian town of Azopa, located on Ossabaw, was attacked and burned.

The Guale reestablished villages and continued to live under the mission system on the islands for another century, cultivating food for themselves as well as contributing to the needs of the mission at St. Augustine, Florida. By the time of the English occupation of the area in the 1730s, the Guale Indians had moved inland, probably in response to the spread of diseases and marauding that took place under the Spanish mission system. In the earliest treaties with the English, Ossabaw was reserved by the Creek Indians as hunting and fishing grounds.

This book begins with the sale of Ossabaw to its first Colonial owner, Grey Elliot, who sold the island to Dr. Henry Bourquin, who then sold it to his son-in-law John Morel. Morel built a house on the north end and profitably farmed and timbered Ossabaw with slave labor. At his death in 1777, Ossabaw was willed to Morel's sons, resulting in four plantations: North End, Middle Place, South End, and Buckhead. The island passed through subsequent owners but was never subdivided beyond the four plantations. Chapter one follows the chain of title for each plantation, illustrated by photographs taken in the 1920s. Some interesting stories and links to local families, as well as Ossabaw's role in state and national events, follow the names of Ossabaw's owners. More detailed information than could be provided here can be found in the Ossabaw Island National Register nomination text and bibliography, as well as in the records of the Georgia Historical Society, the Georgia Department of Archives and History, and other repositories.

Curiously, Ossabaw has always remained sparsely populated. Many of the plantation owners of the 18th and 19th centuries did not establish permanent residency on the island but maintained homes in Savannah, North Georgia, and as far away as New York. Populations peaked during those years, when several hundred slaves worked on Ossabaw's South End plantation. However, unlike on other coastal islands such as Sapelo Island to the south, freed slaves never became landowners on Ossabaw. From the middle of the 19th century until the early 20th century, Ossabaw plantations were farmed on a small scale by their owners or by tenant farmers, including former slaves and their descendants. The resident black population on the island, who had established a church on Ossabaw, relocated as a community to the mainland in the late 1890s. The community is still intact, and the church recently celebrated its centennial. By 1910 the census shows less than 20 people living on Ossabaw, and the legacy of few inhabitants continued when in 1916, the island was reunited under one owner and quickly sold again to a group of wealthy businessmen who used the island as a hunting retreat. These men, who owned homes in Savannah and elsewhere, used the Club House and Boarding House at the North End to house the island manager and guests.

In 1924 Dr. Henry Norton Torrey and his wife Nell Ford Torrey of Detroit, Michigan purchased Ossabaw for use as a family retreat, after their winter home near Savannah was destroyed by fire. The Torreys built the Main House, a Spanish Colonial Revival mansion facing the Ossabaw Sound on the northern end of the island. With their children, William and Eleanor, and a staff of house servants brought down from Michigan, the Torreys enjoyed the island with family and friends, including Henry Ford of Detroit and Howard Coffin of Sapelo Island. Dr. Torrey produced several photograph albums of Ossabaw, which provided the source and inspiration for this book.

William Ford Torrey and his children, William Jr., Annette, Emory, and Randall, took on the challenge of island management in the 1940s and 1950s, including establishing the Circle T Ranch, overseeing timber operations, and working with the Georgia Game and Fish Division to manage the island's deer population.

In 1961 Ossabaw became the site of the internationally acclaimed and attended Ossabaw Island Project, founded by Eleanor Torrey West and Clifford B. West. Some of the world's brightest scholars in many disciplines came to Ossabaw to think, work, and create. The Ossabaw Island Project was one of four programs of The Ossabaw Foundation, the West's private operating foundation, which also sponsored the Genesis Project, Scientific Research, and Public Use and Education programs on the island. With the pressure of rising taxes and development pressure on many of the Georgia islands, the Torrey and West families searched for a suitable steward for Ossabaw. The island remained in the Torrey family until 1978, when it was sold to the State of Georgia as the State's first heritage preserve. The State of Georgia is entrusted with the management of the island's natural and historic resources and works in partnership with The Ossabaw Island Foundation, a public non-profit organization established in 1994 to promote natural, scientific, and cultural study, research, and education on the island, carrying on the mission of the original Ossabaw Foundation. In 1995, the entire island of Ossabaw was listed in the National Register of Historic Places in recognition of its significance to local, state, and national history in areas including archaeology, architecture, agriculture, ethnic heritage, maritime history, and landscape architecture. The National Register nomination form, on file at the Georgia Historic Preservation Division, provided the source for much of the early history recorded in this book and contains an extensive bibliography that will be helpful in future research. The photographs come from the Eleanor Torrey West Collection located at the Georgia Historical Society in Savannah, Georgia, unless otherwise noted. Mrs. West retains a life estate to the Main House and grounds, and remains active in the stewardship of Ossabaw Island.

Like the wind through the trees and the changing tides, what Ossabaw gives is hard to measure. Scientists and artists continue to study and record the island and the ways it supports life, both biologically and spiritually. This book, like a sea shell brought home from the beach, reminds us of the treasures of Ossabaw days present and past, in anticipation of Ossabaw days yet to come.

One

PLANTATIONS

Gen. James Edward Oglethorpe settled at the present site of Savannah in February of 1733. There he was greeted by Yamacraw Indians and their "Mico," or Chief, Tomochichi. Oglethorpe contracted with Mary Muscgrove, daughter of a Creek Indian mother and an English father, to serve as interpreter in his relations with the Native Americans. With her help, a formal treaty was made between the English and the chiefs of a number of Creek Indian tribes, in which the Indians ceded all the lands between the Savannah and Altamaha Rivers, from the ocean to the head of tide water. In that treaty, Ossabaw Island, along with nearby St. Catherines and Sapelo Islands, was reserved by the Indians for use as hunting and fishing grounds. In 1739, as shown in this map, Oglethorpe traveled to Coweta Town, chief city of the Creek Indians, to make a new treaty which reaffirmed Indian rights to the islands. (Courtesy of the Georgia Historical Society.)

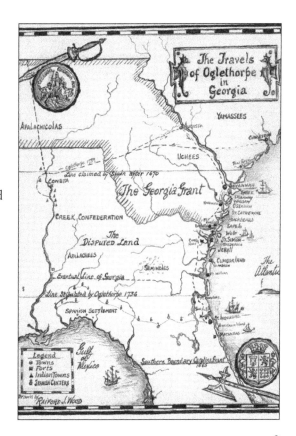

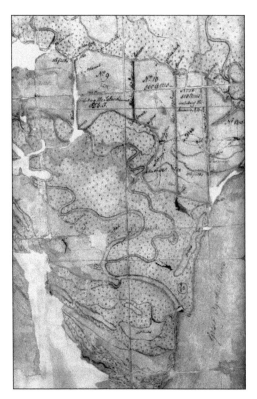

The island of Ossabaw is shown in part in this 1760 survey map. In 1747, an Indian Mico named Malatche, recognized as the Emperor of the Creek territories in a document signed and sealed by 16 other Creek Chiefs, deeded the three reserved islands to Mary Muscgrove Bosomworth and her third husband, Reverend Thomas Bosomworth. Those claims were disputed by both Indian and English factions, and in 1758, a different group of Creek leaders conveyed the three islands to King George II of England. Mary Bosomworth and her husband continued to assert their right to the islands, as well as to petition the colony for payment promised for her services as interpreter.

The English Government directed Henry Ellis, the royal governor of the colony of Georgia, to sell Ossabaw and Sapelo Islands at public auction and use the proceeds to settle the claims of the Bosomworths. The Bosomworths retained their deed to St. Catherines and set up a homestead there. This description of Ossabaw from the survey plat is cited in the original crown grant of Ossabaw Island signed by Henry Yonge and Will DeBrahm, surveyor generals.

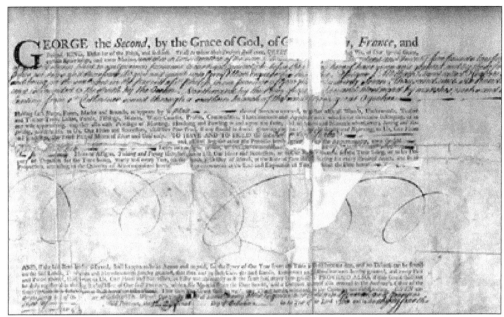

The governor of the colony, with this crown grant from King George II of England, dated October 31, 1760, granted Ossabaw Island to Grey Elliot for £1,325. The document contains the usual provisions of a crown grant, which allows for hunting, hawking, and fowling and reserves to the king of England "all white pine trees, and one-tenth part of the mines of silver and gold." Within the same year, the title to Ossabaw passed from Grey Elliot to Dr. Henry Bourquin, and from Dr. Bourquin to his son-in-law John Morel.

John Morel purchased an undivided half interest in 1760, and the other half in 1763. Carved stone mile markers located along island roads are believed to date from John Morel's tenure on the island. The stone marker pictured here is more ornate than those lining the island's main road. It was found in the woods and may have been a surveyors monument marking a boundary line. (Courtesy of Eleanor Torrey West, private collection.)

This row of live oaks lining the main road on Ossabaw's North End, photographed here in 1924, most likely dates to the Morel period on the island. Morel farmed and harvested timber from the island. After his first wife died, John Morel married Mary Bryan, daughter of Jonathan Bryan, who owned Cumberland Island. In his will, dated June 23, 1774, Morel bequeathed all his cattle, plantation tools, slaves, and the island in equal shares to his sons.

In this 1924 photograph, a man stands atop an enormous pile of timber that awaits pick up at Cedar Dump, one of many historic landings on the island where timber was stockpiled and loaded onto boats. Between 1763 and his death in 1776, John Morel was engaged on Ossabaw in "live oaking," cutting virgin sea island timber for use in ship building. In 1770, he advertised in the *Georgia Gazette* that, "any quantity of Live Oak and Cedar Ship timbers, of any shape and size required" would be cut and delivered "at proper landing on Ossabaw." The *Elizabeth*, one of the earliest ships built in the new Georgia colony, was built on Ossabaw by John Wand.

Pictured here is the North End with the Club House, a late 19th century prefabricated building that is believed to have been erected where the Morel plantation house stood. After John Morel's death the North End was given to Bryan Morel, John Morel's youngest son. In May of 1797 Bryan Morel advertised the North End, describing it as "lands adapted to the cultivation of cotton, indigo or corn—for quantity and quality of live oak timbers, in its wood for excellent and extensive range, for stock of all kinds there is no island in the state, esteemed superior." At his death in 1812, Bryan Morel's son Bryan McQueen Morel, then a minor, inherited the North End. In 1840, he married Louisa Shaw Turner, a granddaughter of Gen. Nathanael Green, late owner of Cumberland Island. Some of their children were born on Ossabaw.

Pictured here is a view from the Club House, looking toward the North End Dock. Bryan Morel and his son Bryan McQueen Morel farmed the property and probably leased it to others to farm. Their children sold the land to James M. Waterbury of New York City in 1886, ending 126 years of Morel-named ownership of Ossabaw. Waterbury sold to an intermediary in 1895, and in 1902 the deed was conveyed to John Wanamaker of Philadelphia. By 1903, Wanamaker representatives had also purchased South End and Middle Place.

This photograph shows a late 19th-century house built at Middle Place, which stood until destroyed by fire in the 1930s. Middle Place is located on Buckhead Creek on the western side of Ossabaw Island. At the death of John Morel, Middle Place went to Peter Henry Morel. He left Ossabaw after his first wife died during childbirth on the island in 1787, selling his share of Ossabaw to David Johnston, who owned half of St. Catherine's Island. From Johnston it went to Sir Patrick Houstoun. At his death, Middle Place went to his daughter Georgia Ann Moodie Houstoun upon her marriage in 1843 to Alexander McDonald.

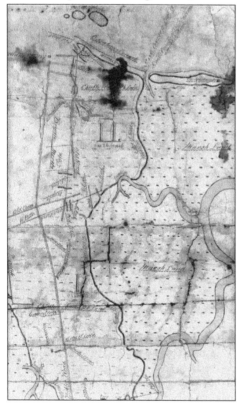

A note on this 1855 survey plat by William Hughes indicates that a mansion stood across from the stone mile marker on the road in front of Middle Place. Now only the tabby ruins of its foundation remain. The McDonalds' daughter Georgia H. McDonald inherited Middle Place and married Charles M. Harper. Harper was reared by his uncle, Col. Alfred Shorter, benefactor of Shorter College in Rome, Georgia. During the Harpers' time at Middle Place, C.B. Moore conducted archeological excavations of some shell mounds, from which vessels and skeletons were uncovered. Harper sold Middle Place to James M. Furber, an intermediary for the Wanamaker family of Philadelphia.

The South End dock and a tenant farm house are pictured in this photograph taken in 1925. South End became the property of John Morel Jr. at the division of his father's estate, and passed through two owners until it was purchased by George Jones Kollock. Kollock maintained detailed plantation diaries, letters, and journals from 1849 until 1861. His records indicate that there were 70 slaves of all ages on the plantation. Kollock sold the South End in the 1870s. It was eventually sold to the Habersham family of Savannah. In 1883 the Habershams sold it to Archibald Rogers, who sold to Carolin C. Maxwell. Maxwell immediately sold the North and South End to William Nevin, representing the Wanamaker interests of Philadelphia.

The Buckhead plantation was farmed into the 20th century, as shown in this photograph from 1924. After John Morel Jr.'s death in 1802, his share of Ossabaw—South End—was divided into two plantations: South End and Buckhead. Buckhead was obtained by his daughter, Mary Anne Morel, who in 1805 married Nathanael Greene Rutherford. Buckhead went to their daughter Mrs. Mary Rutherford Skrine Simmons and finally to her grandson Charles S. Cary. The sale of Buckhead by Charles S. Cary in March of 1916 to Henry Davis Weed ended the Morel descendants' holdings on Ossabaw Island. With this sale, Weed became the first person to bring the island under sole ownership since John Morel died in 1776.

Some of the freshwater ponds on the island show signs of channelization, perhaps for use in rice farming. Old place names and road names still in use today, such as "Rice Pond Road" and "Cabbage Garden Road," indicate the types of crops grown on the island.

The 1860 census indicates that the owners of Middle Place had 69 slaves living in 17 houses. The land was described on the 1855 William Hughes map of Ossabaw as "being adapted to the culture of corn, sugar cane, rye oats, potatoes, peas, etc." and for "the convenience of fishing and hunting."

The tabby slave dwellings, shown in this 1920s photograph, date to the 1840s. During the Civil War, the Georgia islands were evacuated by order of Gen. Robert E. Lee. In 1865, the U.S. Government's Bureau of Refugees, Freedmen, and Abandoned Lands appointed a military governor to reestablish governments on the coastal islands and protect the freedmen and refugees for 30 miles inland. A freedom ship unloaded passengers on Ossabaw that year and found that former slaves had returned and were planting at South End but were living elsewhere on the island. A monthly report noted 78 settlers on Ossabaw at that time. In C.B. Moore's visit to the island in 1896, it was noted that there were a few black families still living at Middle Place. Unlike on other coastal islands, however, freed slaves did not become landowners on Ossabaw. During the 1870s the resident black population formed a church, called "Hinder Me Not" Baptist Church. The minister was Rev. B.O. Butler; there were 68 members. In 1880, the representative of the church was Brother Thomas Bonds. In 1885, the church had 61 members. It moved from Ossabaw to the Pin Point community, south of Savannah. The resident black population is said to have left Ossabaw after a major hurricane in 1898.

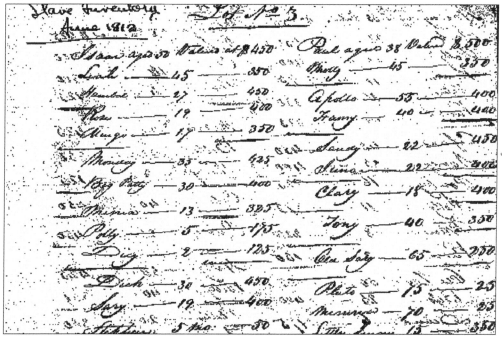

This slave list, dated 1812, is a record of names, ages, and assigned monetary values of individuals from the Morel Plantation. Early 19th-century owners of Ossabaw, including Bryan Morel, Houstoun, Johnston, and Kollock had plantations on the mainland in the Montgomery area. It is likely that slaves on Ossabaw had relatives on the mainland and moved back and forth between plantations, depending upon which sites needed working.

This photograph of the Buckhead house is identified as "The Coolers at Buck Head." By the turn of the century, there were few full-time residents on Ossabaw. A 1916 affidavit notes that there was a house on each of the four main tracts on the island, which were under cultivation.

Pictured here is a man in front of a house at South End. The 1910 census indicates only six people living on the island at that time.

An unidentified man is seen in front of the Club House, c. 1925. The children of Bryan McQueen Morel sold the North End to James M. Waterbury of New York City in 1886, ending 126 years of Morel-surnamed ownership of Ossabaw. Waterbury was characterized as a "leading sportsman" and his sons were international polo players. Waterbury and his wife conveyed the North End to Carolin C. Maxwell of Savannah in 1895. Maxwell sold a few days later to William L. Nevin, who served as president of Wanamaker's stores, in trust for John Wanamaker of Philadelphia. Wanamaker's agents also purchased South End in 1895 and Middle Place in 1903. In 1906 Thomas B. Wanamaker sold North End, South End, and Middle Place to John H. Carr for Henry D. Weed.

Henry D. Weed sold the island to some of the partners in the Strachan Shipping Company, including George P. Walker, George Ferguson Armstrong, Frank Duncan Macpherson Strachan, Harry Garden Strachan, and Robert Walker Groves. These men were active in Savannah and in other coastal endeavors, and used the island for hunting. Mr. Armstrong kept a kennel of hunting dogs at the North End. The superintendent and his family lived in what is called the Boarding House, pictured here in the center of the photograph, to the right of one of the tabbies.

Cyrus Martin, pictured here with a small pig, came to Ossabaw in 1913 at age 13 to work with John Harrison, caretaker of Middle Place for the Strachan Shipping Company. When the company sold the island to Dr. and Mrs. Henry Norton Torrey in 1924, Cyrus Martin and John Harrison stayed on the island to work for the Torreys.

This photograph, dating to the 1930s, shows a group of women in Sunday dress in front of the tabbies on Ossabaw's North End. Originally slave cabins, the tabbies housed island employees up until the early 1980s. The typical work schedule was 10 days on the island, and 4 days off, which afforded employees time to visit with family and friends and attend to business on the mainland.

Two

THAT DEAR OLD PLACE

This sketch of the Main House, built on Ossabaw by Dr. and Mrs. Henry Norton Torrey between 1924 and 1926, shows its rambling Spanish Colonial Revival style, designed in keeping with the Spanish history of the Georgia coast. The *Savannah Morning News* recognized Dr. Torrey's "utmost consideration in doing practically all his business in Savannah," selecting Henrick Wallin and Arthur F. Comer as architects and F. Mcrae as general contractor.

This beautiful portrait of Nell Ford Torrey and her two children, William Ford Torrey and Eleanor Ford Torrey, graces the living room of the Main House on Ossabaw Island. Mrs. Torrey was the granddaughter of John Baptiste Ford, a ship builder. During the Civil War, Mr. Ford went into the glass business and went on to make the first successful pour of plate glass in America. He started the Pittsburgh Plate Glass Company in 1882 at the age of 71, and at 87 he formed the company that later became Wyandotte Chemical Company.

Dr. Henry Norton Torrey, pictured here, was a surgeon and later an administrator of the Harper Hospital in Detroit, Michigan. He served with the Harper Unit in France and Italy during World War I, and continued to be affiliated with the hospital after the war. In 1926, he self-published *The Story of Ossabaw*, a history of the island from records of the Georgia Historical Society and from the abstract of Ossabaw titles.

In 1917, Dr. and Mrs. Torrey purchased "Greenwich," this 40-room home located on the Wilmington River near Savannah. The house and gardens were said to rival the Biltmore Estate in North Carolina. In January of 1923, a fire started and spread throughout the house. Young Eleanor Torrey and her nurse had to jump from a second-story window before a safe passage was found through the attic, allowing the rest of the family, including their grandmother, to escape to safety.

After the fire at Greenwich, the Torrey family continued to spend time on the coast, living on their yacht, the *Tamarack IV*, which was double the size of the later yacht, a 48-footer, pictured here. The *Tamarack IV* was well appointed for comfortable living, and the family was accustomed to life on board, often spending summers on the Great Lakes.

The Torreys spent time with friends on the coast, including the Coffins, who owned Sapelo Island. Pictured here are Nell Ford Torrey, Cornelia Wilder, Mrs. Howard Coffin, Eleanor Ford Torrey, and Howard Coffin on the beach at Blackbeard Island.

The dining cabin and lounge of the *Tamarack* was 15 by 21 feet, equipped with a piano and phonograph. Note the polished woodwork of the walls, furniture, and ceiling and the reflective lights between the windows. The ship was likened to a floating hotel.

Meals for family and guests aboard the *Tamarack* were prepared in this galley, measuring 10 by 15 feet. It was equipped with a six-hole coal range, a hot water furnace for heating the boat, and a large cold storage box operated by two Kelvinator ice machines.

In 1924, the Strachan Shipping Company placed Ossabaw Island up for sale. Nell Ford Torrey's offer of $150,000 was accepted, and Ossabaw became the Torrey family's new winter retreat.

Shown here is the construction of a jetty in 1926. Made from hundreds of wooden pilings, the jetty directs an increased flow of water from the river to the landing at the island's North End. This historic landing, now called Torrey Landing, is situated on a narrow, shallow passage on the south side of the Ogeechee River, just west of two small marsh islands called the Egg Islands. Only one or two pilings remain from the original jetty.

This small work boat, the *Eleanor One*, shown here leaving Torrey Landing, was used to transport supplies back and forth between the mainland and the island. In 1929, Dr. Torrey purchased a lot on the Burnside River in the Vernon View neighborhood. A cottage on the lot was built for Robert L. Mercer, uncle of renowned singer and songwriter Johnny Mercer. The property provided a docking point and access to the island from the mainland.

This aerial photograph, facing north, shows the North End of Ossabaw with the tabbies, Boarding House, Barn, the Club House, and the field with its row of live oaks. A long causeway, planted in cabbage palm trees, leads to the Torrey landing, the North End dock.

This aerial photograph of the Main House shows its placement on the northeast side of the island, approximately one mile east of Torrey Landing and about a half-mile south of the previous photograph. The site for the house was chosen for its sweeping view of Ossabaw Sound to the north and the sheltering woods for Mrs. Torrey's gardens to the south.

Here two unidentified workers assess the progress of construction amidst piles of bricks and other materials. To the left side of the men is the exterior of the two-story living room, shown before the pink stucco finish was applied. To the right of the large arches are the openings for living room windows. The large rectangular opening awaits the placement of a plate glass window, which was a tribute to Nell Ford Torrey's grandfather John Baptiste Ford and his accomplishment of making the first successful pour of plate glass in America.

In this photograph, the scaffolding is in place in preparation for placement the Ludiwici roof tiles. The stacks of milled lumber in the foreground were purchased in Savannah and shipped by barge to the island. Construction workers roomed in the Boarding House at the North End while working on the Main House.

The Torrey family enjoyed cookouts and picnics at the beach while the Main House was under construction. Here the yacht captain, J.F. Wicks, takes a turn as chief cook.

Gatherings on Ossabaw were much more informal than the grand affairs held at Clairview, the Torrey's home in Grosse Pointe, Michigan. Nevertheless, Mrs. Torrey, pictured second to the left in the hat, scarf, and dress, hosted a picnic "in style" with the help of an aproned cook and her butler, Andrew Speed, who was properly attired in a white shirt and black necktie.

Ossabaw Island was a place for family and close friends to relax and enjoy the outdoors. In this photograph, a marooned timber makes a suitable bench for Mrs. Torrey and Mrs. Fetty of Savannah.

Here young William (Bill) Ford Torrey's riding gear earned him the nickname "Bill Hart," after an early silent screen star. Note Bill's horse, Prince, wearing a hollow-seated McClellan saddle.

The two-story great room of the Main House was completed in 1926, with an exposed wooden beam ceiling and paneled and plastered walls. Trophies from Dr. Torrey's hunting trip to Africa line the walls and a beautifully painted mural of the island hangs above the fireplace, showing the island's main roads and plantation sites. The colorful painting captures the shape of Ossabaw's shoreline in 1924 when ocean sands stretched the length of the island. Over the decades, tidal rivers have divided the Ossabaw coastline into three separate beaches.

Here, Dr. Henry Norton Torrey, Eleanor Ford Torrey, Mary Reynolds, and Nell Ford Torrey enjoy a fire in the inglenook of the stone fireplace, where cozy seats and bookshelves lined with fascinating titles are an inviting place to relax.

The dining room has a beautiful blue-tiled floor, and the fireplace and bay window are finished with face tiles imported from Portugal, Spain, and Italy. Recessed lights were used to set the table, and dining was always by candlelight. Mrs. Torrey brought trunks filled with linens, silver, and china to grace the table at Ossabaw. Inside and outside help accompanied the Torreys to Ossabaw from Grosse Pointe, Michigan, including a cook, a waitress, a butler, upstairs and downstairs maids, a housekeeper, and a chauffeur.

Warmed by its southern exposure, the sunroom is decorated with Oriental-style woodwork and draperies with up-cast lighting from the chandeliers. Beyond the French doors of the room, a solarium opens out onto the patio and gardens. Also opening out onto the patio, down the hall from the sunroom, are two guest bedrooms with hand-painted shutters and decorative tile work.

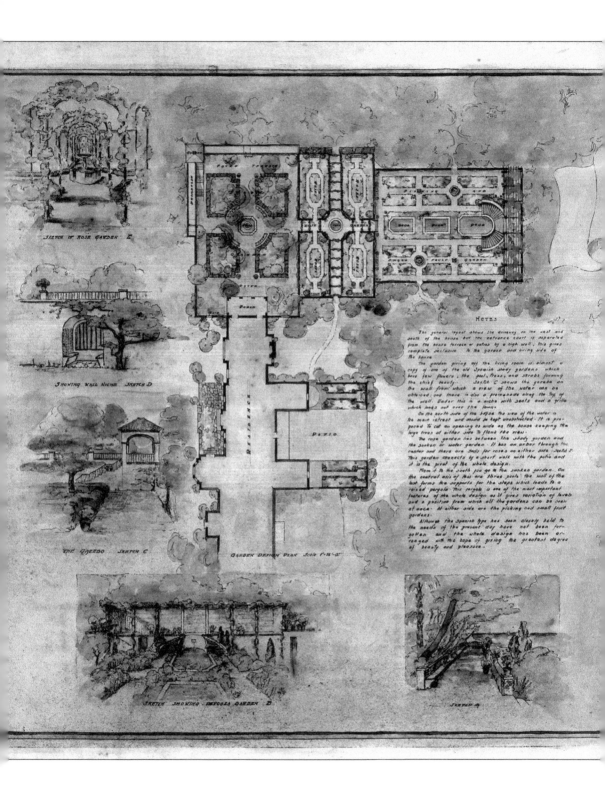

SKETCH OF ROSE GARDEN E.

SHOWING WALL NICHE SKETCH D

THE GAZEBO SKETCH C

GARDEN DESIGN PLAN SCALE 1"=16'-0"

NOTES

The general layout shows the driveway on the west and south of the house but the entrance court is separated from the house terrace or patios by a high wall, this gives complete seclusion to the garden and living side of the house.

The garden giving off the living room is almost a copy of one of the old Spanish shady gardens which have few flowers, the pool, trees, and shrubs forming the chief beauty. Sketch C shows the gazebo on the wall from which a view of the water can be obtained; and there is also a promenade along the top of the wall. Under this is a niche with seats and a grille which looks out over the lower.

On the north side of the island the view of the water is the main retreat and should be kept unobstructed. It is proposed to cut an opening as wide as the house keeping the large trees at either side to flank the view.

The rose garden lies between the shady garden and the sunken or water garden. It has an arbor through the center and there are beds for roses on either side. Sketch E. This garden connects by a short walk with the patio and it is the pivot of the whole design.

From it to the south you get to the sunken garden. On the central axis of this are three pools, the wall of the last forms the supports for the steps which leads to a raised pergola. This pergola is one of the most important features of the whole design as it gives variation of levels and a position from which all the gardens can be seen at once. At either side are the picking and small fruit gardens.

Although the Spanish type has been closely held to the needs of the present day have not been forgotten and the whole design has been arranged with the hope of giving the greatest degree of beauty and pleasure.

SKETCH SHOWING PERGOLA GARDEN B

SKETCH A

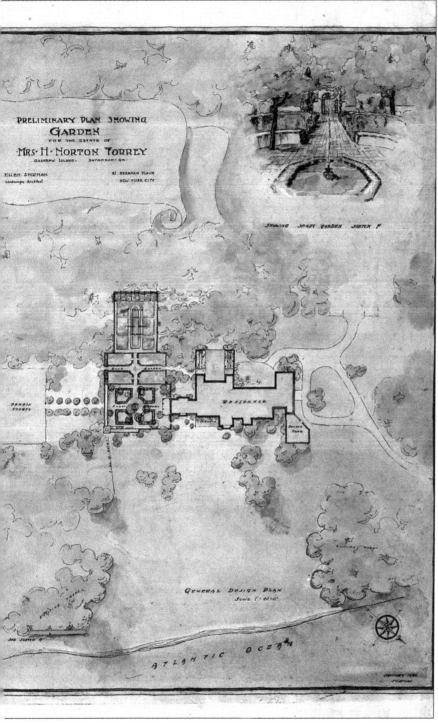

The original plan for the Main House gardens was designed by Ellen Biddle Shipman, a pioneer in landscape architecture in the early decades of the 20th century. Shipman trained women in architecture and landscape at two alternative schools at a time when major university programs were closed to them. The first garden made for the Main House at Ossabaw was the patio garden, enclosed on three sides by the pink stucco walls of the house and flanked by twin gardens, terminating in twin tile fountains. Later gardens were planned by Mrs. Torrey, and are featured in *The Garden History of Georgia*. (Courtesy of Elrod Sims.)

Eleanor Ford Torrey and her longtime friend Mary Reynolds converse on the terra cotta tile of the patio garden. In the center of the patio is an aquarium, 15 feet in circumference, where silver and gold fish swam in the sunlight.

The grounds of the Main House were maintained as lawns under native live oak trees, giving a sweeping view of the Ossabaw Sound. The gardens in the back of the house were accessed by broad steps leading from the patio to a camellia garden and large beds of azaleas and drifts of spring bulbs and pansies. (Courtesy of William Ford Torrey Jr., private collection.)

The playfully proud figure of Peter Pan surveys the water garden from a raised mound at the head of the stream. From here water flowed over a rocky spillway past iris, ferns, and violets to a large pond below. (Courtesy of the Cordray-Foltz Collection at the Georgia Historical Society.)

Dr. Torrey, Eleanor Torrey, and Mary Reynolds survey the pond from a decorative bridge spanning the lower pond. Behind them is a small boat enjoyed by family and guests. In the center of the pond was a small island with sculpted cement trees.

In this photograph, Nell Ford Torrey (far left) poses next to her sister Stella Ford Schlotman, enjoying a spring day on the lawn in the company of a sportingly dressed gentleman and two well-dressed ladies. (Courtesy of Patricia Schlotman Carmel.)

The lawn and gardens were an inviting place for a spring picnic. Pictured on the left are Stella Schlotman and Nell Ford Torrey, sitting across from Eleanor West's cousin, Patricia Schlotman. The table is set with Mrs. Torrey's china—brought down from Grosse Pointe, Michigan—and decorated with flowers from the garden. Mrs. Torrey employed a gardener at Ossabaw, an Englishman named Mr. Strouffer, who raised flowers in greenhouses and managed crews that maintained the landscape. (Courtesy of Patricia Schlotman Carmel.)

Opera singer Lily Pons, star of the Metropolitan Opera and films such as *I Dream Too Much* with Henry Fonda, visited Ossabaw. With her husband, conductor Andre Kostelanetz, Lily Pons made appearances on the *Bell Telephone Hour* and *Voice of Firestone* radio programs and was one of the highest-paid performers of her time. As shown in this photograph, taken on the patio of the Main House, Lily Pons was known for her great style off-stage as well as onstage.

Henry Ford was the Torrey's first guest on Ossabaw, penning his signature in the guest book in 1926. Mr. Ford was a "happy acquaintance" from Michigan and neighbor on the coast, owning a plantation in nearby Richmond Hill. A great fan of square dancing, Mr. Ford brought records on one of his visits to Ossabaw and played them on the Torrey's Victrola phonograph. The table in the Main Hall was removed, and family, guests, and house servants joined in the dance. (Courtesy of Eleanor Torrey West, personal collection.)

The Torrey's staff from Michigan rode down ahead of the family to prepare the house while the family often took the train. A garage behind the Main House sheltered the automobiles used on Ossabaw including a rugged Ford station wagon used for hunting trips and this 1928 Packard touring car used for chauffeured trips from the house to the beach. (Courtesy of William Ford Torrey Jr., private collection.)

Counted among the influential friends and guests visiting Ossabaw was President Calvin Coolidge. One of Georgia's early governors is pictured here with "LuluBelle," a stylish maiden made of wax. Dr. Torrey was known for a lively sense of humor and enjoyed practical jokes. One of his favorite pranks was hiding LuluBelle in the guest room, startling unsuspecting guests. (Courtesy of Patricia Schlotman Carmel.)

Pictured here next to an unidentified man holding a large boar is Mrs. Betty Mitchell, Island Manager John Harrison, and Cyrus Martin. Mrs. Mitchell was the wife of famous World War I Gen. Billy Mitchell, whose statement that military strategists should look to airplanes rather than cavalry and ground troops earned him a court martial. General Mitchell was posthumously recognized for his foresight. Mrs. Mitchell's hunting companions, Harrison and Martin, worked on the island prior to the Torrey's arrival in 1924 and provided invaluable assistance in coping with the many challenges of island life.

In this photograph dated December 1926, a group of men are gathered before a hunt at the South End in front of a house and barn. Pictured here, from left to right, are John Harrison, two unidentified men, Howard Coffin of Sapelo Island, Alfred W. (Bill) Jones of Sea Island, and two unidentified men. The man on the first mule is identified as Paul and next to him is Cyrus (Jimbo) Martin.

Pictured here after a successful hunt are a young Bill Torrey and Howard Coffin of Sapelo Island (both kneeling) and Dr. Torrey, standing on the far right.

Barbecues were an anticipated event on Ossabaw. In this 1929 photo, these men prepare roasted duck over an open pit fire. In the background is the house at Middle Place, which burned to the ground a few years after this photograph was taken in 1929. (Courtesy of Patricia Schlotman Carmel.)

While her parents entertained friends in the house and gardens and hosted hunting parties, Eleanor Ford Torrey enjoyed exploring the island on horseback with her cousins, Josephine and Patricia Schlotman. On the far right of the photograph is Miss Haskins, Eleanor's governess. (Courtesy of Patricia Schlotman Carmel.)

Here, Eleanor and her cousins are dressed for island adventures. In this small bateau, an unidentified island employee steadies the boat with a long paddle. The girls prepare to launch out into the tidal creek at low tide, perhaps on a mission to gather oysters. (Courtesy of Patricia Schlotman Carmel.)

The family spent from January to May on Ossabaw. The children's tutors helped them keep up with their studies, balancing the call to outdoor adventures on the island. Pictured here is Eleanor at age 16 with a book in hand next to her cousin Josephine Schlotman. (Courtesy of Patricia Schlotman Carmel.)

The beaches of Ossabaw are wild and beautiful examples of the natural processes that take place on barrier islands. In this photograph, Eleanor Torrey and her friend Mary Reynolds look eastward in front of trees shaped by the wind.

YACHT TAMARACK

GENTLE HINTS FOR GUESTS

PLEASE DON'T   WEAR HOBNAILS ON DECK. IF YOU INSIST UPON THIS YOU WILL HAVE TO WALK ON YOUR HANDS.

PLEASE DON'T   TRY TO IMPRESS US BY TAKING FREQUENT BATHS. FRESH WATER ON A SALT WATER YACHT IS AT A PREMIUM

PLEASE DON'T   WORRY THE PLUMBING WITH MATCHES AND CIGARETTE STUBS. THE ENGINEER HAS ALL HE CAN DO IN THE ENGINE ROOM.

PLEASE DON'T   CUT THE TOWELS WITH YOUR RAZOR. IT MAKES MRS. TORREY FURIOUS.

PLEASE DON'T   SHAVE AND TAKE A BATH AFTER MEALS ARE ANNOUNCED. DO IT BEFORE. WE HAVE BREAKFAST AT 9 A.M., LUNCHEON 1 P.M., DINNER 7 P.M., WEATHER PERMITTING. IN BAD WEATHER WE FURNISH ROLLS ONLY.

PLEASE DON'T   LEAVE YOUR CABIN WINDOWS OPEN IN ROUGH WEATHER. GET YOUR SHOWERS IN THE BATH ROOM.

PLEASE DON'T   TELL US YOU HAVE NEVER BEEN SEASICK. SAVE YOUR BREATH AS YOU MAY NEED IT.

PLEASE DON'T   COME ABOARD WITH A GOOD LIQUOR APPETITE UNLESS YOU HAVE GOOD LIQUOR TO ACCOMPANY IT. WE ARE FOR VOLSTEAD—WITH RESERVATIONS.

Dr. Torrey is pictured standing alone in the center of this busy scene of men readying the *Tamarack IV*, docked at Torrey Landing.

Dr. Torrey's sense of humor shines through in this list of rules for the *Tamarack*. The list reveals much about life on board the yacht, from the dining schedule to the many demands upon the engineer. It also shows Mrs. Torrey's attention to detail in providing for her guests. "Please don't wear hobnails on deck" cautions guests not to wear heavy shoes that could scratch the well-polished wood. "We support of the Volstead Act, with reservations," refers to the Act of Congress prohibiting the sale of alcoholic beverages, passed in 1919 and repealed in 1933. (Courtesy of William Ford Torrey Jr.)

On March 29, 1928, an explosion rocked the *Tamarack*. The blast, caused by a spark from a vacuum, destroyed the boat and blew off the roof of the boat house at Torrey Landing where it was docked. The steward on board at the time suffered serious burns, but survived.

Gar Wood, builder of the Torrey's last two yachts, is pictured with one of his inventions, which was made during his retirement in Miami. As a boy, Gar Wood raced the ferry boats captained by his father. He grew up to design and build American power boat race winners and began to make his fortune when he invented the hydraulic lift. Gar Wood specialized in luxury racing boats, while his partner, Chris Smith, who went on to form the Chris Craft boat company, focused on building more affordable work boats. Gar Wood's plant switched to making boats for the military during World War II. (Courtesy of Eleanor Torrey West, private collection.)

This yacht, one of two built for Dr. Torrey by Gar Wood, was 48 feet long. With twin 1500 liberty aircraft engines it would run at 50 miles per hour. This last *Tamarack* to be owned by the family was loaned to the coast guard in World War II. Unfortunately, the yacht was run aground in local waters. (Courtesy of Patricia Schlotman Carmel.)

Three

COMING OF AGE

In this photograph dated 1938, Nell Ford Torrey greets an arriving party of family and friends. Son Bill Sr. attends to the automobile, next to his daughter Annie, sister Eleanor, son William Jr., and wife Margaret Annette Baker Torrey. In the dark dress and feathered hat is Trina French, the children's godmother. (Courtesy of William Ford Torrey Jr.)

William Ford Torrey attended Princeton University and went on to work with Wyandotte Chemical Corporation, founded by his great grandfather, Jean Baptiste Ford.

Eleanor Ford Torrey married John Shallcross in 1935. Mr. Shallcross was recruited after college by Dr. Charles Holmes Herty, inventor of the technology needed to produce fine quality paper from Southern Pine. They moved to Savannah and were able to make frequent visits to the island.

Bill Torrey is pictured here with Bert Cremers and cousin Emory M. Ford, associates at Wyandotte Chemical Corporation, a company that processed and sold alkalis for use in a variety of household and industrial products.

Nell Ford Torrey enjoyed creating festive tables, as in this photograph of Easter Lunch in the dining room in the 1940s. Mrs. Torrey is seated at the head of the table at the far end next to her sister, Stella Schlotman. From left to right are William Ford Torrey Sr., Mary Reynolds, Annie Torrey, Gillian Shallcross, Michael Shallcross, Stella Ford Schotman, Nell Ford Torrey, an unidentified maid, Eleanor Torrey Shallcross, Joseph Schlotman, and William Ford Torrey Jr. (Courtesy of William Ford Torrey Jr.)

Like their father, Bill Torrey Sr.'s children were introduced to horseback riding at an early age. From left to right are chauffer Wally Dacon, Annie Torrey, friend Bill Crow, Bill Torrey Jr., and Bill Torrey Sr. In the background are the row of tabby houses with children playing out in front. (Courtesy of William Ford Torrey Jr.)

Randy Torrey shows off his catch in the courtyard of the Main House. In the background is the Crosley, a small gas-powered car used to motor around the island by parents and children alike. (Courtesy of William Ford Torrey Jr.)

In a setting of wind-shaped trees by the beach, young Annie and Bill Jr. and a family friend gather on the hood of the car between Mame and Wally Dacon. Dacon was Nell Ford Torrey's chauffeur and is remembered as having a flare for drama that entertained the children. (Courtesy of William Ford Torrey Jr.)

In his self-published book, *The Story of Ossabaw*, Dr. Henry Norton Torrey wrote, "The primitive and original atmosphere of Ossabaw has always been maintained, and the property today retains its natural beauty and charm." He ends the story with, "I hope that I have given some idea of the history and fascinations of this dear old place." Dr. Torrey died in 1945. The photograph and poem on the following page were reprinted from his book. (Courtesy of William Ford Torrey Jr.)

Nell Ford Torrey pictured here with daughter Eleanor Shallcross and grandson Michael Shallcross, continued the tradition of coming to Ossabaw every winter. She enjoyed adding to and walking in the gardens, sharing the beauty of the island with friends, and spending time with her children and grandchildren.

"Ossabaw"
by Carlyle McKinley

Far from thy shores, enchanted isle,
   Tonight I claim a brief surcease
From toil and pain, to dream awhile
     Of thy still peace.

To wander on thy shining strand
   And lose awhile life's troubled flow;
Its tumults die upon thy sand,
     Blest Ossabaw.

Here care ebbs out with every tide,
   And lose awhile life's troubled flow;
The heart looks out on life clear-eyed,
     And finds it good.

On that fair land, on that still sea,
   A spell of mystery lies,
And all the thoughts they wake in me
     Are mysteries.

Once more I stand upon thy shores,
   How peaceful yon far world doth seem,
A willing exile evermore,
   Here on Ossabaw let me dream.

At the time of this photograph, taken in 1953, William "Bill" Torrey Sr. had remarried. His new wife, Helen Brauner Torrey, was a writer whose article in *The Saturday Evening Post* chronicled the efforts to manage the overpopulation of deer on Ossabaw. Included was the discovery of a tranquilizing dart made from nicotine used to drug deer so they could be captured and relocated. Ossabaw deer were relocated to War Woman Dell in North Georgia. The young boy pictured on the left is Randy Torrey. (Courtesy of William Ford Torrey Jr.)

Bill Torrey Sr. built this house, called the Little House, a few hundred yards east of the Main House. Helen Brauner Torrey's unpublished manuscript entitled "The Silent Shore" describes life on the island where she learned to hunt deer and duck and was introduced to low country boils and barbecues put on by island employees. (Courtesy of William Ford Torrey Jr.)

Lucille Williams, pictured here with her son Emanuel, worked on Ossabaw year-round with her husband Emmanuel (pictured below), while Mrs. Torrey's staff from Michigan came to work only for the winter months and returned to their duties at Clairview in Michigan after the Easter season. Lucille remained a longtime family friend. (Courtesy of Eleanor Torrey West, private collection.)

Cyrus Martin, Bill Torrey Sr., and Emmanuel "Mannie" Williams are pictured here in wet wading boots in the courtyard of the Main House after a successful duck hunt. (Courtesy of William Ford Torrey Jr.)

Bill Torrey Sr. established a number of ventures in an effort to produce revenue from island resources. The most successful of these was in timber—primarily pine—for lumber and pulp. A forester was hired to "cruise" the timber, selecting trees to be thinned for new growth and trees to be left standing within sight from the roads. Large saw dust piles at the South End and at Middle Place are remnants from this enterprise. This photograph of two unidentified men with island-milled timber was dated 1938, taken during earlier timbering operations on the island. (Courtesy of William Ford Torrey Jr.)

Ossabaw oysterbeds, shown in this photograph from the 1920s, were leased to a seafood packing firm in Savannah for a percentage of the gallon price. Part of the agreement was that oyster beds be built up by reseeding.

When Bill Torrey Sr. took on the management of Ossabaw, several hundred head of wild cattle lived on the island, such as these photographed in 1924. Cows and pure-bred bulls were brought to the island and the herds increased dramatically. Riders were hired to round up cattle for branding, tagging, and checking for diseases. The early days of the business, named the Circle T Ranch, were lucrative, but later, problems with drought and the expense of feed and transport proved costly.

Pictured here in 1952 on top of the hay is B.G. Pinckney, head of the cattle operation. Miles Pinckney, island superintendent (with hands on his hips) stands between two unidentified workers. (Courtesy of William Ford Torrey Jr.)

Dr. and Mrs. Torrey had a small beach house built, pictured here in 1938. The house was located at the eastern end of the Willows Causeway, near the intersection of Bradley Road. The beach house was the destination for many picnics and cook-outs and provided a changing spot for beach-combers and ocean swimmers. (Courtesy of William Ford Torrey Jr.)

By 1948 the ocean had eroded the shoreline right up to the Beach House, eventually claiming its prize. The picture window was removed and fitted into the north side of the Club House.

A new beach house was constructed, reportedly by Mrs. Torrey's English gardener, Mr. Stouffer. Note that the walls are made from the trunks of cabbage palm trees. But once again, the ocean currents shifted inland, threatening the fate of the mid-island shelter. (Courtesy of William Ford Torrey Jr.)

Here, Bill Torrey Sr. and his youngest son, Randy, inspect the sandy bank, anticipating the inevitable approach of the sea. Since this photograph was taken in 1953, sediments have filled in the area, creating a marsh that blocks the ocean tides. A new sand beach has formed one half mile to the east. (Courtesy of William Ford Torrey Jr.)

Mr. and Mrs. Miles Pinckney and Mr. and Mrs. Marc Sawyer strike a pose at the edge of the marsh in this photograph dated 1952. Mr. Pinckney was island superintendent and Mr. Sawyer was the boat captain.

Pictured here in 1962 is "The Shop" where routine repairs to island vehicles and equipment were made. (Courtesy of William Ford Torrey Jr.)

As a teenager, Bill Torrey Jr. worked the Ossabaw cattle ranch. He went to Cornell University, and Duke graduate school, majoring in forestry. After he married, he and his family continued to use the island as a family retreat, where they hunted, fished and enjoyed the beach. Bill is pictured here on the left with his friend T.S. Medernach, after a duck hunt.

In one of Ossabaw's tidal creeks, young William Ford Torrey III catches his first fish. His sister, Elizabeth Torrey, holds the pole, alongside his proud mother, Marta Bender Torrey.

Nell Ford Torrey is pictured under "the Big Oak," one of the largest trees on the island, located near the South End Beach. A National Geographic team estimated the tree's age to be 600 years.

In this photo, Mrs. West's young friend, William Foskey, waters the plants in Nell Ford Torrey's beautiful patio garden.

Four

THE OSSABAW ISLAND PROJECT

Tex Schewitz, longtime friend and supporter, participant, and board member of the Ossabaw Island Project tends to his sculpture of a circling shark on its pedestal in the front lawn of the Main House. The Ossabaw Island Project was established in 1961 as the first program of The Ossabaw Foundation. The project invited people of creative purpose in many disciplines from many states and nations to work and find inspiration on the island of Ossabaw. (Courtesy of Eleanor Torrey West, private collection.)

Clifford West was associated with the Cranbrook School in Michigan and had been inspired by the vision of its founders, G.C. Booths and Anna Scrips Howard, in establishing a school for the arts. He invited his friend David Dodge, author of *To Catch a Thief*, to come to Ossabaw to explore the possibility of using Ossabaw as a place for fostering creative work and ideas. All agreed it would be a likely success. Friends who had associations with the American Academy of Art in Rome, including Tex Schewitz and Samuel Barber, gave their support, and in 1961, the Ossabaw Island Project began. (Courtesy of Eleanor Torrey West, personal collection.)

When Eleanor Torrey West, pictured here with her husband, Clifford West, and sister-in-law Ann Wood, inherited an undivided half interest in the island of Ossabaw, she wanted to share it without destroying that which makes it so special. (Courtesy of Eleanor Torrey West, private collection.)

Eleanor Torrey West and Clifford Bateman West established The Ossabaw Foundation, which funded the Ossabaw Island Project. Project members were provided with private rooms and comfortable surroundings at the Main House and Little House. Outbuildings and some of the rooms in the Main House were renovated into work spaces including a pottery and piano studios, a weaving room, and a photography lab. Writers often worked in their bedrooms or at tables on the patio. (Courtesy of Eleanor Torrey West, private collection.)

Breakfast was served at 7 a.m. and provisions for lunch were laid out so members could have lunch on their own. The rest of the time, each person was free to work with no demands or interruptions. A formal dinner was served at 6:00 p.m., followed by coffee in the living room, at which time the diverse mixture of artists, scientists, philosophers, writers, and business people shared their work and had the opportunity to interact with and learn from one another.

Roman Jakobson was a professor of Slavic languages, literature, and linguistics at Harvard University, Massachusetts Institute of Technology, and College de France (Paris). Professor Jakobson, who spoke 13 languages, wrote "Nowhere else did my studies reach such a high degree of concentration, intensity, and clarity as on Ossabaw Island where I have repeatedly worked as a Fellow of the indeed magnificent Project. The peculiar ground and geographical contour of this island act as an inspiring background of our scientific theories and artistic imagination."

Krystyna Pomorska, literary critic, is pictured here with husband Roman Jakobson and Captain Roy of Ossabaw. During her stay on Ossabaw, Pomorska chose to work on the landing of the main stairs, writing a criticism of Pasternak, giving the cozy nook the name, "Dr. Zhivago's corner." (Courtesy of Eleanor Torrey West, private collection.)

H.W. Janson, professor of fine arts at New York University and author of the classic text, *The History Of Art*, wrote, "I look upon Ossabaw as a unique and uniquely valuable resource. The Ossabaw Island Project makes it possible for artists, scholars and scientists to pursue their work, to exchange ideas and to refresh their spirits under ideal conditions." (Courtesy of Eleanor Torrey West, private collection.)

Pulitzer Prize winner Ralph Ellison, author of *Invisible Man*, pictured here with his wife, Fannie McConnell Ellison, enjoyed the wide expanse of the Ossabaw shoreline during a visit to the island in 1971. Ellison served on the Board of advisors of the Ossabaw Island Project, helping to promote the project among artists and scholars in many disciplines.

Conversations between people from different disciplines in the exotic atmosphere of Ossabaw Island evoked a chemistry that helped people to see their work and the world from new and different perspectives. The founders of the Ossabaw Island Project believed this type of exchange to be essential in forging solutions to some of the world's most challenging problems. Through the project, Ossabaw became the setting for scores of conferences, workshops, and meetings for groups including the Porter Institute, Xerces Society, Southeastern Center for Photographic Arts, and the Southern Writers Conference. (Courtesy of Helen Hamada.)

Pictured here in 1961 are William Saltzman and Lois Ober Miller hosting a clothesline show of Saltzman's paintings produced during their stay on the island. Freelance writer Lin Root remarked, "Just as the fantastic flora of Ossabaw put forth roots and shoots, and multiply; so the writers, painters, sculptors, composers, scientists, scholars, and project members of every type find their work taking on new dimensions, expanding in unforeseen directions."

Sculptor Harry Bertoia counted his Ossabaw stay as a high point in his life experience. He wrote, "from the practical viewpoint, it triggered a new approach to bronze casting." Understatedly, Bertoia continued, "This is meaningful when we look back and find nothing new had happened to bronze casting for thousands of years." His first piece, *Ossabaw Echoes*, is at the Cranbrook Museum of Art in Michigan, and his largest sculpture is at Dulles International Airport. The sculptor said of Ossabaw, "Far more precious was sensing my faculties expanding and bringing me one inch closer to nature's offerings." (Courtesy of Eleanor Torrey West, private collection.)

Lillian Holm, head weaver and textile designer at Cranbook, is pictured here in the loom room, originally the servants dining room of the Main House. Here, she experimented with weaving natural materials found on the island.

In the summer of 1971, scientists from Yerkes Primate Research Center introduced four laboratory-raised chimps onto Bear Island, a 100-acre island on the western side of Ossabaw, to determine the feasibility of establishing breeding colonies of the endangered animal. During the experiment the chimps abandoned the shelter built for them and began making nests in the trees, grooming each other for ticks, and eating native vegetation. One infant was born during the experiment, but did not survive. This chimp was the first free born chimp in North America. One of the chimps, named "Jiggs," is pictured here next to a fenced food drop. (Courtesy of Eleanor Torrey West, private collection.)

Many chapters in Ossabaw's history lie buried beneath centuries of leaves, mud, and sand. These old nails and broken plates and bottles, fragments of pipe stems, and pottery shards were found eroded out of a creek bank, and mark a site used by humans over the past several centuries, as well as thousands of years ago. The locations Ossabaw's shipbuilding industry in the 18th century and the late 19th-century African-American community church and dwellings on Ossabaw are still a mystery. Someday, archaeologist and historians may locate these and other sites and be able to piece together more about the lives of Ossabaw's early inhabitants. (Courtesy of Ann Foskey.)

In 1972, the University of Florida and the University of Georgia conducted a large-scale, long-term research and conservation project on the endangered Loggerhead Sea Turtle. Members of the Ossabaw Foundation's Genesis Project participated in the research, walking certain sections of the beach each night and searching for females crawling from the sea to lay their eggs. The turtles were tagged and measured, and the eggs were moved to a hatchery constructed for protection from raccoons, feral pigs, and other predators. Later research determined that moving turtle eggs can alter the sex of the embryos. Since that discovery was made, nests are rarely moved, and screens are placed over the nests in an effort to limit predation. (Courtesy of Elizabeth Lynes Adams.)

As the Loggerhead Sea Turtle project grew, a camp was created to house student researchers. Screened tents on wooden platforms were set up, and the camp was given the name, "Turtle Town." When the State of Georgia purchased the island in 1978, the Department of Natural Resources assumed responsibility for the continuation of turtle research on the island. (Courtesy of John Earl.)

Dr. Eugene P. Odum, author of *Fundamentals of Modern Ecology*, documented the invaluable life-support functions of marshlands and estuaries as ocean food chain producers, waste cleansers, and tidal energy absorbers. Dr. Odum was a longtime trustee of the Ossabaw Foundation and supported early ideas to preserve Ossabaw Island as a "self-maintaining eco-system" that would serve as a resource for environmental study, research, and education. (Courtesy of Eleanor Torrey West, private collection.)

More than half of the territory encompassed by Ossabaw Island is made up of wide expanses of marshes laced with tidal creeks. Spartina marsh grass covers this acreage like a vast prairie that is a home and a nesting ground for all forms of life, from shrimp and crab to alligators and storks. The marshes form the base of a vast and intricate food chain supplying fish, birds, and human beings with sustenance and livelihood. Changing from radiant green in spring and summer, the marshes transform into the "golden isles" of fall and winter. (Courtesy of Paul Efird.)

In 1965, a population of 11 free ranging Sicilian donkeys was established on Ossabaw Island, obtained from a herd on Bull Island, South Carolina. In 1975, the males of the herd were captured, vasectomized, and released in an effort to control the growing population. A few pregnant females gave birth to male donkeys, and the population began to increase once again. In 1980, Genesis member Bill McCort of Pennsylvania State University conducted doctoral dissertation research on the donkeys, studying their social organization on their island habitat. Currently the remaining population of donkeys is being removed from the island and individuals are being relocated to mainland homes. (Courtesy of John Earl.)

This fire screen, designed and crafted by artisan Ivan Bailey, represents the feral pigs that have been a part of Ossabaw's history for more than 400 years. Descendants of escaped domestic swine brought by the Spanish explorers, the feral swine of Ossabaw Island have remained virtually isolated from subsequent hybridization. The pigs have been the subject of periodic studies for more than 30 years by I. Lehr Brisbin of the Savannah River Ecology Laboratory and others. Published scientific studies of the feral swine of Ossabaw have documented unique biological and biochemical characteristics and adaptations that may contribute to research in medical and other sciences. As a non-native introduced species, however, the large population of pigs has an adverse effect upon some of the native island eco-systems and current management plans include efforts to eliminate the pigs from the island.(Courtesy of Ann Foskey)

Beautiful and evocative photographs were produced by artists including Nancy Marshall, John Earl, and Sally Mann. James Valentine and Robert Hanie worked on Ossabaw while creating the classic volume, *Guale, the Golden Coast of Georgia.* Here photographer Nancy Blackwell chooses a subject among the palmetto fronds on the forest floor. (Courtesy of John Earl.)

Sculptor Ira Matteson benefits from the natural lighting and solitude provided in this renovated studio.

Writer Olive Ann Burns works at her typewriter in the Little House. During her stay on Ossabaw, a fellow project member and linguist from Tel Aviv was captivated by her colorful southern colloquialisms, such as "let me love your neck." He asked if she had considered writing a book. She had, in fact, and that evening after dinner, Olive Ann Burns read the first chapter from a book she was working on entitled, *Cold Sassy Tree*. Other famous writers of the Ossabaw Island Project include Annie Dillard, Rosemary Danielle, and Margaret Atwood. (Courtesy of Helen Hamada.)

"Ossabaw provides the privilege of solitude; the comfort of kinship; a deep response to the strange power of the Island; and more, much more that nourishes the spirit and makes it fruitful," wrote Lin Root. Here, Haia Lawrence, Carol Halstead, Patricia Poole, and Saturn Davis perform an Ossabaw-inspired dance.

Peter Paul Kellog, professor of ornithology and biological acoustics at Cornell University, pictured here with Jill Schleminger and Larry Payne, wrote that Ossabaw "is a place where artist and naturalist may receive fresh inspiration, which is a basic ingredient of creativity." (Courtesy of Paul Efird.)

Willard Trask, prolific translator of works such as Casa Nova's autobiography and the trials of Joan of Arc, was a beloved Ossabaw Island Project Member. (Courtesy of Eleanor Torrey West, private collection.)

Bates Little, photographer for *National Geographic*, works at the marshes edge where tracks of heron, raccoon, and deer wind through the mud among a myriad of fiddler crab holes. (Courtesy of John Earl.)

Artist Susan Senserman set up a portable studio selecting the southern exposure of the patio for an afternoon of painting. (Courtesy of John Earl.)

Shari Brush and Lorraine McCarty show their work in this photograph taken from an upstairs balcony overlooking the patio of the Main House. Colors and shapes of Ossabaw's forests, dunes, and marshes were captured on canvas and formed the inspiration for more work after the artists left the island.

Five

MAKING IT WORK

For eight months out of the year, the Ossabaw Island Project filled the Main House with guests. James Brownlee was one of 18 staff members who worked to beautify and maintain the Main House and grounds, an environment that made such an impression on all who visited the island. (Courtesy of Eleanor Torrey West, private collection.)

Here, Anne Wood, Clifford West, and Chuck Wood take a day away from the Main House and get out to explore the island. Anne and Chuck Wood were Ossabaw Island Project Directors, and participated in recruiting and selecting participants and coordinating logistics and transportation. On Sunday, after a week of intensive work and study in their studios at the Main House, project members would take a trip to the beach.

Eleanor Torrey West was active in the management of Ossabaw Island and the programs of the Ossabaw Foundation. As the project grew in scope and size, she benefitted from the talents of full-time administrative assistant Wendy Hunter Higgins (not pictured). Mrs. West is pictured here wearing a boar tusk necklace made by archeologist Charlie Pearson, with Al Bradford, one of the Ossabaw Island Project Directors. (Courtesy of Eleanor Torrey West, private collection.)

Carol Burdick, poet and writer, professor of English and composition, and former Ossabaw Island Project member, became Ossabaw Island Project co-director in 1979. Affectionately known as "C.B.," she assumed responsibilities of fund-raising and handled the logistics of bringing project members to the island. (Courtesy of Eleanor Torrey West, private collection.)

Photographer, musician, and professor John Earl, longtime trustee and project member, creates a self-portrait. John Earl shared his appreciation for coastal environments while teaching the skills of photography. John Earl's photographs of the Georgia Coast have been featured in *Guale the Golden Coast of Georgia* and he also authored a children's book on John Muir. (Courtesy of John Earl.)

Pictured here from left to right are Eugene Graves, Arthur Graves (holding the grand champion of New Mexico Appaloosa stallion "Star"), and Eleanor Torrey West. Arthur Graves served as island manager beginning in 1951 and his brother Eugene later succeeded him. In addition to managing cattle operations on the island, they raised horses as well.

Roger Parker, pictured here in front of one of the tabby houses on the North End, came to work on Ossabaw in 1951. He worked with his uncles in managing Ossabaw's cattle and wild pig population and later assumed the role of island manager. Roger's brother Stanfield Parker maintained vehicles, equipment, and roads and captained the boats. Stanfield went on to work for the Department of Natural Resources on the island until his retirement in 2000. (Courtesy of Eleanor Torrey West, private collection.)

The Ossabaw Island Project provided a rare opportunity for its participants—space and time to work unhindered by the demands of daily life. This gift was made possible by the hard work of a dedicated full-time staff and the personal resources and generosity of Eleanor Torrey West. Queenie Mae Williams and Sarah Parker, anchors of the Main House staff, are pictured here with Mrs. West by the front door of the Main House. (Courtesy of Eleanor Torrey West, private collection.)

Off-island contractors, such as long time friend Richard Boaen, pictured here, provided special services needed on the island such as repairing roofs, working on generators and boilers, and helping prepare for groups and special events. (Courtesy of Ann Foskey.)

During the early days of the Ossabaw Island Project, though Eleanor Torrey West's children were in school and establishing careers, all served on the board of advisors. Gillian Ford Shallcross, now with the Boston Museum of Fine Arts, continues to serve in an advisory capacity on the board of the newly formed Ossabaw Island Foundation. (Courtesy of Eleanor Torrey West, private collection.)

Justin P. West, Eleanor Torrey West's youngest son, is pictured here at a young age on a cart with his pony, King. As a college student, Justin built and equipped the pottery studio for the Ossabaw Island Project, and later, his film production company produced two documentary films, *Ossabaw Island* and *Traces of Passage* used in fundraising efforts for the Ossabaw Foundation. One of the island roads, King's Way, was created when the pony, King, darted off through the woods with Justin and cart in tow. (Courtesy of Eleanor Torrey West, private collection.)

Michael Torrey Shallcross, Mrs. West's eldest son, worked for more than five years as island manager and managing director of the Ossabaw Foundation. For 21 years Eleanor Torrey West had funded the Ossabaw Foundation out of her own personal resources. As financial advisor, Michael spearheaded the efforts to find outside sources of funding for the foundation's programs, which proved difficult. In 1982, the Ossabaw Island Project came to an end due to lack of funds. (Courtesy of Eleanor Torrey West, private collection.)

As a teenager, John Post Shallcross worked on Ossabaw during the summers, mending roofs and repairing roads under island managers Arthur and Eugene Graves. John applied his hands-on approach and knowledge of the island by serving as the director in the second year of the Genesis Project, the land-based independent study program centered at Middle Place. (Courtesy of Eleanor Torrey West, private collection.)

Queenie Mae Williams, pictured here with Ossabaw Island Project member Roman Jakobson, first came to the island with her husband, who worked for Dr. Torrey. She later worked at the Main House during the period when William Ford Torrey was operating the Circle T Cattle Ranch. She continued working at the Main House, cooking for the Ossabaw Island Project. (Courtesy of Eleanor Torrey West, private collection.)

Eleanor Torrey West lived in the Club House while the Ossabaw Island Project was in operation at the Main House. Pictured here are Queenie Williams, Mrs. West, and long-time Ossabaw resident, Cyrus "Jimbo" Martin. (Courtesy of Eleanor Torrey West, private collection.)

Pictured here are Queenie Mae Williams holding young Benjamin Wohlauer, Eleanor Torrey West's grandson, along with James Brownlee and Cyrus "Jimbo" Martin at an Easter luncheon on the island. (Courtesy of Eleanor Torrey West, private collection.)

Pictured here from left to right are Agnes Graves Moody (wife of Arthur Graves), Eleanor Torrey West, and Liz Graves (wife of Eugene Graves). Both Agnes and Liz managed housekeeping operations for the Main House during the years of the Ossabaw Island Project, while their husbands served as island managers. These women added support, strength and joy to the project and shared those qualities with those who came to live and work on the island.

Since the establishment of the Ossabaw Foundation in 1961, Eleanor Torrey West has committed personal energy and resources to make Ossabaw available to people of creative thought and purpose to work and study on the island. In addition to her groundbreaking work in supporting interdisciplinary education and natural resource conservation, Mrs. West maintains her life-long love and enjoyment of animals, supporting the humane treatment of those that have been abandoned or mistreated. This photograph, taken by Heather Brown, represents Mrs. West in the Shorter College Hall of Fame. She is pictured with her horse Maria.

Eleanor Torrey West is pictured here with a pig named Maria Bosomworth and a dog named William Rodgers, the main characters in a true story about the friendly relationship between the two animals. Documented and written by Mrs. West, the book, entitled *Maria Bosomworth and William Rodgers*, was published in 1976 by the Beehive Press in Savannah and won an Award of Excellence in the Southern Book Competition of the Southeastern Library Association. It was republished in 1990 by the Darien News and continues to be a favorite story among audiences young and old.

This universal symbol was painted on the door of the Club House for the benefit of island pigs, much to the chagrin of the hefty bovine in the photograph below. Feral pigs have been an integral part of Ossabaw Island for 400 years. Mrs. West occasionally tamed wild pigs, who rapidly became accustomed to mealtime. (Courtesy of Eleanor Torrey West, private collection.)

Cyrus "Jimbo" Martin was born in 1900. The son of a former slave, Jimbo grew up on Skidaway Island. He came to work on Ossabaw in 1913 with John Harrison and continued to live and work on Ossabaw for 70 more years. Speaking in the Geechee dialect, he shared recollections of "old timers" and old ways with his son Cyrus Martin Jr. of Savannah, who was born on Ossabaw in 1933. Jimbo died in 1995 at the age of 95. (Courtesy of John Earl.)

Six

THE GENESIS PROJECT

The Genesis Project was established at Middle Place in 1970 on an old plantation site on the Buckhead Creek. For more than a decade, the Genesis Project provided a place for independent study in a near wilderness environment. During its first season, Genesis members converted old lumber camp shacks and barns to provide housing for the project. Water was drawn from an artesian well and an outdoor shower was constructed. In the next season, running water was piped into the cook shack. In this photograph, students work to convert the old stables into rooms for project members. (Courtesy of Eleanor Torrey West, private collection.)

Students worked 20 hours per week with the daily chores of life at Middle Place, as well as working with island employees in areas such as cattle management, road and building maintenance, and vegetable growing and freezing. Here, Mrs. West walks the long rows of the freshly tilled garden sowing seeds for a new season's crop. (Courtesy of John Earl.)

In the fall of 1972, the Genesis became a year-round program. The average length of stay for a participant was two months, during which time they shared the responsibilities of planting, tending, or harvesting the vegetable garden, depending upon the season. The rest of the time was spent working on independent study projects. Pictured here on the left is painter Judi Barber, who went on to become the Director of the Hambidge Center in North Georgia. (Courtesy of John Earl.)

94

On Cook Day, one or two Genesis members would handle all the chores and prepare the meals for the day, freeing the other participants to pursue their studies. Pictured here from left to right are Evan Landolt, Al Bradford, and Michael Hamburger, preparing a large batch of tea. (Courtesy of Al Bradford.)

Work on Cook Day included milking the cow, gathering eggs from the chickens, harvesting honey, and working in the garden. Pictured here is "Daisy," one of several milk cows serving the Genesis Project. (Courtesy of Helen Hamada.)

A spirit of cooperation prevailed as students applied their unique talents to benefit the community. Some built simple dwellings such as the Horse Field Tree House, pictured here, where one project member wrote his doctoral thesis for a Ph.D. in philosophy. (Courtesy of John Earl.)

Living without electricity, participants adopted a schedule of waking at sunrise and working until sunset. While many Genesis members were engaged in research that was island focused, others brought work with them and found quiet and solitude that enabled them to complete major projects. (Courtesy of Al Bradford.)

Genesis artists worked in media including ceramics, photography, painting, drawing, and filmmaking. Here Evan Landolt paints in the company of Naomi Fuches in the horse field Tree House. (Courtesy of Al Bradford.)

At Genesis, students found time to experiment with new ways of doing things, from making pottery out of island clay to the making of a sailboat, as in this photograph with Bob Lobis. (Courtesy of Al Bradford.)

The treehouse over the marsh captures the spirit of adventure and innovation that characterizes the Genesis Project. Beneath the branches, the tide rises and falls twice a day, and breezes blow across a wide expanse of marsh. Genesis co-director Helen Hamada reflected how students took a week or two to acclimate to life at Middle Place, then seemed to thrive in their work and in their interactions with other project members. (Photo by Nelson C. McClary; Courtesy of Al Bradford.)

On occasion, Genesis members would load up the project vehicle—a Volkswagon bus—and drive across the island to the beach. Here, M. Hickman enjoys some solitude among the driftwood trees on South Beach. (Courtesy of Al Bradford.)

The Genesis Project afforded students time to explore and discover, reflect upon and be inspired by the diversity of plants and animals of a barrier island eco-system. Here, naturalist Scott "Muskrat" Pendergrast shares a rare close encounter with a fallen hawk. (Courtesy of Helen Hamada.)

The tidal creeks flowing in and out of coastal marshlands are teeming with life. In 1965 Dr. Eugene Odum and scientists working on Sapelo Island estimated that 95% of all ocean food spends part of its life cycle in the marsh. Bob Burns of nearby Daufuskie Island made cast nets and showed Genesis members how to use them. Fresh fish, crabs, and shrimp that were caught on the banks of Buckhead Creek made up a large part of the diet of Genesis members. (Courtesy of Helen Hamada.)

This tabby structure, photographed several years after the Genesis Project ended, was originally the foundation of the two-story, turn-of-the-century house at Middle Place. The structure was renovated for use as housing for Genesis members. All the accommodations at Genesis were simply furnished with a bed, a desk and a chair, a wood stove for heat, and oil lamps for light. (Courtesy of Emily Earl.)

Buckhead Creek at high tide provides a beautiful setting for this photograph of a Sweat Lodge, shown here with Genesis Co-Director Al Bradford and Project Member Stephen Shoenholtz. (Courtesy of Helen Hamada.)

Helen Hamada, pictured here firing Raku pottery with Brian Donovan, was a Genesis participant and returned to co-direct the project from 1976 to 1980. Directors provided stability and continuity for the influx of students who entered and left the project at different times throughout the year. Responsibilities of directors included soliciting and reviewing student proposals, fundraising, procuring supplies and groceries from the mainland, and coordinating of building and maintenance activities. (Courtesy of Helen Hamada.)

The garden provided an abundance of vegetables, including perennial crops of asparagus, horseradish, and rhubarb. (Courtesy of John Earl.)

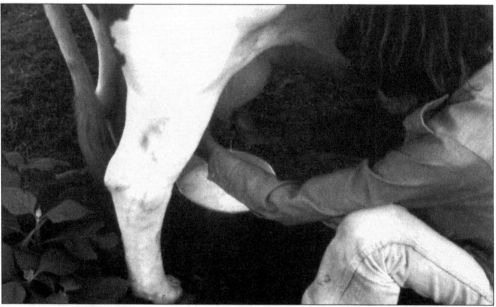

Pictured here is John Earl, milking Daisy, who gave two gallons of milk every day. Milking the cow was a part of the learning experience at Genesis. Daisy was patient with newcomers, but if the milking wasn't going as fast as she would like, she was known to wait until the bucket was nearly full, then kick it over. Filmmaker Ross McElwee was awarded a fellowship to attend the Genesis Project, where he produced scenes from his film *Sherman's March*, featuring Daisy and Wini Wood, a project member studying linguistics who grew fond of the cow. (Courtesy of John Earl.).

Pictured here several years after the project ended, the Cook Shack stood under the shading branches of a giant live oak tree. The Cook Shack was the gathering spot at the end of long days of research in the field or in the trees. (Courtesy of Emily Earl.)

Project members gathered in the Cook Shack for dinner, reporting on events of the day. One can imagine the interesting conversations exchanged as members came in from tracking feral pigs, identifying island plants, observing donkeys, tagging turtles, feeding chimpanzees, or researching birds. David Bayne spent his days in a tree blind-observing egrets. Pictured here from left to right are Jim Elicker, Thea Johannos, unidentified Genesis members, and Genesis Co-Director Al Bradford, far right. Johannos prepared her Master's degree thesis on Ossabaw's feral Sicilian donkeys. (Courtesy of John Earl.)

The Tower House, pictured here under construction, had living and studio space for two people with additional space in the central hall for storage and a studio. In 1979 and 1980 Genesis members used a newly acquired portable chainsaw mill to cut lumber from island oaks downed by Hurricane David. Using post-and-beam construction from hand-hewn timers, the Tower House frame was built and pine siding applied to the exterior.

A workshop held in 1980 taught Genesis members useful skills in historic restoration projects, as used by Michael Billa, Genesis co-director, pictured here. Participants of the workshop milled the timber and cut the joints for a new outhouse. (Courtesy of Helen Hamada.)

No nails were used in the frame of the Tower House at Middle Place. Here, Genesis Co-Director Helen Hamada uses a drill to prepare a timber that will be secured with wooden pegs.

In 1979 a solar shower and sauna was built from hand-hewn timbers using post and beam construction, and the roof was made of hand-split cedar shakes. Along with David Bayne, (standing on top of frame) Genesis members raise the frame in the company of Mrs. West and early State of Georgia Department of Natural Resources personnel. In 1980 a solar water-heating workshop was held resulting in the addition of a solar water heater that supplied hot water for the Genesis community. (Courtesy of Helen Hamada.)

Attention to beauty as well as practicality was evident in the work of the Genesis project. Here David Bayne and Mary Earl prepare to install the stained glass window in the solar sauna and shower. (Courtesy of John Earl.)

In winter months, Genesis participants would linger in the Cook Shack after dinner sharing the days events, discussing ideas, and reading out loud. Not only was it an enjoyable way to pass the evening hours in a season of early darkness, but it was also a way to conserve firewood, since most of the wood at Genesis was cut using a two-person saw. Pictured here, from left to right, are Bob Lockhart, Bill McCort, Al Bradford, three unidentified Genesis members, and Florence Long and Phil Long of Penn State. Bill McCort was a Genesis member who wrote his doctoral dissertation on his study of the social behavior of feral Sicilian donkeys on Ossabaw Island. (Courtesy of Helen Hamada.)

Seven

THE SALE

In 1958 Eleanor Torrey West and her brother's children, William Ford Torrey, Annette Torrey Fraser, Emory Mead Torrey, and Randall Ford Torrey, inherited undivided half interests to Ossabaw Island. The Torreys' interest was held in the corporate structure of Ossabaw, Inc. The responsibility of owning and managing an island as large as Ossabaw was overwhelming to all involved. For the decade of the 1960s, the programs of the Ossabaw Foundation operated on the island with a lease and use agreement from Ossabaw, Inc. But by 1970, the family's concerns about the increasing financial burden of mounting taxes were realized when local taxes jumped 500 percent in one year. (Courtesy of John Earl.)

Eleanor Torrey West and her children sought a solution that would preserve the island that had been loved and cared for by their family for close to 50 years. For eight years they entered discussions with conservation groups; federal, state and local governmental agencies; and private citizens looking for a solution. (Courtesy of Eleanor Torrey West, private collection.)

The families looked at what was being done on other islands and consulted with friends and business associates. Pictured here on the beach after a flight over the island are Thomas McCabe, chairman of the board of Scott Paper Company; Bill Torrey Jr.; and local pilot Sam Baker. Friend A.W. (Bill) Jones of the Brunswick pulp and paper mill took the picture. (Courtesy of William Ford Torrey Jr., private collection.)

Here the Torreys host the Ossabaw, Inc. board meeting on the island. Among the guests seated for dinner in the dining room of the Main House were, from left to right, Richard Scarlett (attorney), Annette Torrey Fraser, Mrs. Kostrevagh, Marta Bender Torrey, Andrew Kostrevagh (C.P.A.), Janet Scarlett, and Dick Sisung (National Bank of Detroit). (Courtesy of William Ford Torrey Jr., private collection.)

The great grandchildren of Dr. Henry Norton Torrey and Nell Ford Torrey were in attendance with their friends, the Scarletts, at the 1971 board meeting of Ossabaw, Inc. Pictured around the barbecue pit from left to right are Jan Scarlett, Sam Torrey, Dick Scarlett, Beth Torrey, Brian Peck, Stephen Scarlett, and Torrey Peck. (Courtesy of William Ford Torrey Jr., private collection.)

Jack Crockford (left), head of Georgia's Game and Fish Division, is pictured with Sam Candler of Cumberland Island and the Natural Areas Council. Crockford was involved in the discussions regarding the sale of Ossabaw to the State of Georgia. He had worked with the Torrey family over the years, conducting research in managing the island deer population. (Courtesy of William Ford Torrey Jr., private collection.)

While governor of Georgia, Jimmy Carter visited Ossabaw Island. In this gathering in the living room of the Main House, Governor Carter meets with the family to discuss the possible sale of the island. Carter encouraged the family to consider the State of Georgia as a suitable steward for Ossabaw. (Courtesy of Eleanor Torrey West, private collection.)

Eleanor West, pictured here with Gov. Jimmy Carter, retained a life estate to the Main House and grounds, which she inherited from her mother, Nell Ford Torrey. Under a use agreement with the State of Georgia, the Ossabaw Foundation continued its programs on the island. For several years, the details of a sale to the State of Georgia had to be worked out. The island was appraised at $16 million. The family donated $8 million toward the sale, with special restrictions on how the island would be used. The State of Georgia would pay $4 million. A donor for the remaining $4 million was found in philanthropist Robert Woodruff. (Courtesy of Eleanor Torrey West, private collection.)

Pictured here on the beach at Ossabaw are William Ford Torrey Jr., Governor Jimmy Carter, Randall Ford Torrey, and Emory Mead Torrey. The sale of Ossabaw to the State of Georgia was finalized in 1978 under Gov. George Busbee. Not pictured is the Torrey's sister, Annette Torrey Fraser. (Courtesy of William Ford Torrey Jr., private collection.)

This photograph shows the beautiful South Beach of Ossabaw at low tide, with neighboring St. Catherine's Island in the distance. On June 15, 1978, George Busbee, governor of Georgia, signed an executive order dedicating Ossabaw Island as a heritage preserve, "to protect, conserve, and preserve the natural and cultural resources of this Island for the benefit of present and future generations, and that Ossabaw Island shall only be used for natural, scientific, and cultural study, research, and education, and environmentally sound preservation, conservation, and management of the Island's ecosystem, under conditions carefully monitored and controlled by the Department of Natural Resources." (Courtesy of Ann Foskey.)

Habitat for wildlife, including the ancient species of reptile the American Alligator, is secured in the protection of Ossabaw Island. (Courtesy of Ann Foskey.)

Low intensity prescribed burns are one management tool used to prevent excessive build up of underbrush and to stimulate new plant growth to enhance wildlife foraging. (Courtesy of Ann Foskey.)

The Department of Natural Resources identifies and protects sensitive habitats, such as this dune area on Middle Beach. Rare species found on Ossabaw include loggerhead sea turtles, piping plovers, Wilson's plovers, Peregrine falcons, American oystercatchers, bald eagles, wood storks, least terns, and gull-billed terns. (Courtesy of Ann Foskey.)

Management of Ossabaw includes annual hunts for a variety of game species, including white-tailed deer. (Courtesy of Ann Foskey.)

The Ossabaw Island Foundation raises and administers funds for the rehabilitation of historic structures on the island, including the 19th-century Club House, pictured here. The Club House now provides housing and workspace for individuals and groups pursuing natural, cultural, or scientific study, research, and education.

The Department of Natural Resources personnel maintain island roads and infrastructure. In 2001, electric power from the mainland was brought to the island for the first time via underground cables, leading to the retirement of the island's long-used, diesel-powered generators. The Georgia Historic Preservation Division maintains a file of historical information about the island and provides technical support in identifying and protecting historic and archaeological resources on the island, such as this row of live oaks, believed to date to the 18th century.

In 1994, a newly formed public non-profit foundation called the Ossabaw Island Foundation was established. The Ossabaw Island Foundation "encourages natural, scientific, and cultural study, research, and education on Ossabaw Island, and conserves and protects Ossabaw Island's unique resources, in partnership with the State of Georgia for the benefit of present and future generations." (Courtesy of Ann Foskey.)

Eight

PUBLIC USE AND EDUCATION

The Public Use and Education program on Ossabaw grew out of the belief that people must be allowed to experience wild lands in order to appreciate and understand the importance of preserving them. From 1961 through 1994, the Ossabaw Foundation hosted educational groups who camped in the island's wilderness setting or held conferences at the Main House. Applications required the presence of qualified leadership and encouraged pre-trip preparation for participants. Groups provided their own curriculum while on the island, in fields such as art, botany, coastal ecology, science education, scouting, and social work. Since 1995, this program has continued through the non-profit organization, the Ossabaw Island Foundation, under a use agreement with the Department of Natural Resources. (Courtesy of John Earl.)

Camping conditions on Ossabaw are primitive, and groups must bring everything they need. On-island staff transport groups to one of several designated campsites and provide drinking water. In addition to tents, lanterns, food, and clothes for all types of weather, groups bring their own curriculum and the supplies needed for study in that discipline. This group of biologists from Shorter College brought field guides, nets, seines, and microscopes, to get a close-up look at island life. (Courtesy of Dr. M. Craig Allee.)

A barrier island is made up of multiple eco-systems, including beaches, dunes, interdune meadows, marshes, fresh water ponds, and maritime forests. Each environment supports a diversity of plant and animal life that has adapted to the conditions of that setting. Here, students study the maritime forest with its live-oak trees, Spanish moss, Resurrection fern, mosses, and lichens. (Courtesy of Dr. M. Craig Allee.)

An encounter with total darkness is a novel experience for many people. Far away from the lights of the city, the Ossabaw experience draws people together around a campfire, and rekindles the arts of conversation, storytelling, and song. (Courtesy of Paul Efird.)

After a night spent sleeping on the ground, students gather for a breakfast of grits under a parachute. The parachute serves as a cook tent or shelter over a campfire, providing a dry place to cook meals out of the inevitable wind and rains of early spring. In 1999 a tin-roofed cook shelter, called the Shorter Shelter, was built at this camp site at the end of Willows Road. (Courtesy of Paul Efird.)

The water for campers came from an artesian well, located a quarter of a mile from the campsite at the Willows Field. The water is pumped from a well drilled in the 1950s, which taps the aquifer, now 100 feet below the surface. This Shorter student starts the pump and bathes quickly in cold water on a cold day. (Courtesy of Paul Efird.)

Among the primitive facilities on Ossabaw Island is the privy. The "Half Moon Hotel," pictured here, was built by Shorter College students. (Courtesy of Paul Efird.)

A designated cook day worked well for large groups of students staying more than a few days on the island. Small groups of students would plan and cook one day's meals for the entire group. On this day, students would cook breakfast and pack picnic lunches for the others, who were free to work on independent projects. Here, a student cooks pancakes over the campfire. (Courtesy of M. Craig Allee.)

Students walk along the edge of the marsh, along a field of Spartina, the predominant marsh grass on the island. Spartina is able to live in high salt environments in soil that is high in sulfur. It forms part of the marine food chain, providing food for microorganisms that in turn feed fish and shell fish. (Courtesy of M. Craig Allee.)

Independent projects are an important part of the time spent on Ossabaw. Students select projects in any number of areas, including botany, zoology, chemistry, geology, or a combination of disciplines, as this one where a student studies the depth and composition of marsh sediments. (Courtesy of Paul Efird.)

Dr. Philip Greear and his colleagues in the biology department at Shorter College in Rome, Georgia have been bringing students to Ossabaw Island since 1969. Dr. Greear, who retired from teaching in 1985, was a trustee of the Ossabaw Island Foundation and a member of the Genesis Advisory Board. A botanist and ecologist, Dr. Greear had a style of teaching that encouraged students to explore and enjoy natural environments. He helped students develop an understanding of natural processes and inspired many to pursue careers in biology and environmental sciences. (Courtesy of Eleanor Torrey West, personal collection.)

Many puzzling objects wash up on barrier island beaches, sometimes after being in the sea for decades. Other times, the sea erodes layers of beach sand, revealing remnants of old marsh mud buried beneath. Here a student investigates an interesting discovery with Dr. Jim Colbert. (Courtesy of M. Craig Allee.)

Ossabaw is a place where few humans have tread and one can imagine what life must have been like for primitive people. (Courtesy of Paul Efird.)

Here students learn how to harvest some of the bounty of the marshes, perfecting the skill of throwing a cast net. (Courtesy of Dr. M. Craig Allee.)

Much of Ossabaw's upland areas are second growth forests recovering from the live-oaking of the 18th century and the pine harvesting of 19th and 20th centuries. Many of the live-oak trees are hundreds of years old, and some specimens have been estimated to be more than 600 years old. On a hike with friend and photographer Paul Efird, Ann Newman Foskey and Andrew Kemp, as undergraduates at Shorter College, size up a magnificent live-oak tree. (Courtesy of Paul Efird.)

Ossabaw's tidal creeks are teeming with life, providing a nursery and feeding ground for saltwater animals such as this blue crab. (Courtesy of Paul Efird.)

Once groups are transported from the dock to their campsite, walking is the mode of transportation. Here, Todd Stoner, Dr. M. Craig Allee, and Linda Allee of Shorter College walk Ossabaw's South Beach, a six-mile round-trip hike from their camp site in the middle of the island. (Courtesy of Dr. M. Craig Allee.)

Access into a tidal creek is not as easy as it appears. Here, Jerry Stephens is initiated into island life as he sinks into saturated marsh mud. In the background, Greg McKibben and Daniel Price use their feet to feel for clams at low tide. (Courtesy of Paul Efird.)

The campers warm up around the fire with coffee and hot chocolate as the winds blow across the marsh behind Middle Beach. Included in this picture are Julie George, Linda Allee, Todd Stoner, and Ann Payne. (Courtesy of M. Craig Allee.)

After a week on Ossabaw, somber Shorter students leave the island on the *Eleanor IV*, filled with memories that will last a lifetime. In the article "Enchanted Isle" in *Historic Preservation* (the National Trust for Historic Preservation magazine, November/December 1995), Jane Brown Gillete posed the following question, pondered by many who love and care for wild places: "How do we interact with the wilderness and still keep it wild?" The last private owners of Ossabaw maintained this invaluable balance for more than half of the 20th century. They made sure by the restrictions and conditions of the sale of the island to the State of Georgia that this delicate and imperative harmony would not be destroyed, but preserved, setting a course that will guide Ossabaw Island into the future, free to work its magic and reveal its many treasures. (Courtesy of Paul Efird.)